MW01282450

Prayers for Each Moment

100 Conversations with God
About Real Life and Real Stuff

TAMA FORTNER

Ink &
Willow

Contents

PRAYERS FOR MOMENTS OF SORROW AND STRUGGLE

PRAYERS OF WINS, WORRIES, AND BLESSINGS

PRAYERS OF QUESTIONS AND CONFUSION

PRAYERS FOR LIFE'S MESSY MOMENTS

PRAYERS FOR ALL I'M FEELING

PRAYERS FOR LOVING OTHERS WELL

PRAYERS OF JOY AND PRAISE

PRAYERS TO PRAY TOGETHER

Thank You, Abba,
for who You are
and for all You've done.
Forever and always,
with all that I am,
thank You.

Before You Begin

PRAYER.

AT ITS ESSENCE, PRAYER IS A CONVERSATION.

A GIVE-AND-TAKE.

A LISTENING AND LEANING IN.

It's a conversation about anything and everything. About little things and monumental things and all the endless things in between. Prayer is taking everything to God and learning to have a conversation without end.

One verse that is written on my heart and mind and that never ceases to fill me with wonder is Hebrews 4:16: *"Let us come boldly to the throne of our gracious God. There we will receive his mercy, and we will find grace to help us when we need it most."*

Do you see that? The open invitation? The God of all creation is inviting me—you, each of us—to step into the throne room of His presence. We don't have to creep in or slip in, hoping not to be noticed or worrying we might take up too much space. No, God invites us to walk in boldly as His beloved children, as co-heirs to His kingdom, as if we belong. Because He has, in fact, made a way for us to belong there with Him.

And so we are welcomed into His presence. To have a conversation with Him. Or to simply be still with Him.

Because prayer isn't a transaction; it isn't about the asking or the getting.

Instead, prayer is an opportunity to abide—to live and move and have our being—in the very presence of God.

Does that sound a bit daunting or even intimidating? It doesn't need to be. There's no need for worry or fear in prayer. You don't have to work at the words or say them all just right.

Prayer simply—and wonderfully and divinely—connects the branches of our lives to the Vine, where we are nourished and nurtured and encouraged to grow into all He created us to be.

In these pages, you'll find a collection of prayers. They aren't fancy or formal. They're echoes of my own conversations with God. Raw and honest and real. They often begin with questions and confusion, then end in trust as I talk things through with Him.

I hope they touch your heart and inspire conversations of your own.

Turn to the prayer you need, open to one at random, or read them straight through from beginning to end. It doesn't really matter. What matters is that you step into the throne room. God is waiting there for you. And He'd love to talk with you for a while.

With love and prayers for you,

Tama

PRAYERS FOR THE DAYS, TIMES, AND SEASONS

When the Day Is Beginning

Let me hear of your unfailing love each morning,
for I am trusting you.
Show me where to walk,
for I give myself to you.

PSALM 143:8

HOLY FATHER, THANK YOU. Thank You for this beautiful new day, for Your breath of life that fills my lungs, and for this fresh start.

As my feet hit the floor, guide me to the places where I should go today and to the people You would have me meet. Fill my mind with thoughts of You and my mouth with the words You would have me share.

Teach my heart to take up the servant's cloth, just as Jesus did, and to serve where I can and those I can.

Protect me from the evils of this world and the evils of my own wayward will, which we both know is probably the greater danger.

Open my eyes to see You at work in the world around me. Give me the courage, the desire, and the love for others to join You there in that work.

And more than anything, God, draw me closer and closer and still closer to You. Hold me safe in the circle of Your grace always.

I love You, Lord.

Amen.

When Savoring a Cup of Coffee or Tea

Give thanks to the LORD, for he is good!
His faithful love endures forever.

1 CHRONICLES 16:34

BEAMS OF SUNSHINE SLIPPING THROUGH CLOUDS, butterflies landing whisper-soft on blooming flowers, and this cup of sweet warmth in the cool of the early morning . . .

Lord, it's these little things that so often make me smile. These little gifts from You.

This warm mug between my hands anchors me here in *this* moment. This *present* moment with You.

Each sip reminds me of Your goodness—a goodness that sweetens all the moments of my life. Its soothing trail of warmth down my throat calls to mind the life-giving, rejuvenating waters of Your presence. Let me drink deeply.

Thank You, God, for cool, quiet mornings and warm cups of comfort. For Your goodness and grace. For inviting me to meet with You here and linger here in the soothing, sustaining comfort of Your love.

Amen.

When Sitting Down to Eat

My God will meet all your needs according
to the riches of his glory in Christ Jesus.

PHILIPPIANS 4:19, NIV

THANK YOU, FATHER, FOR THIS FOOD, for this table, and for this place to share it in. And thank You for the precious ones gathered here . . . even when it's just You and me. Or perhaps especially when it's just You and me.

Forgive me for the times I forget to say thank You. It's so easy to take this for granted—food without worry, without uncertainty over when my next meal might come.

I look around and see all You have given me. Yes, there are times when I selfishly wish I had more. And there are times when I realize how ridiculously blessed I am.

You take care of me, God. You provide everything I truly need. Every day You lay out a feast for me . . . for my body, heart, and soul.

So, thank You, Lord. I praise You for this food and for all You do for me.

Amen.

When Waiting

They who wait for the Lord shall renew their strength;
they shall mount up with wings like eagles;
they shall run and not be weary;
they shall walk and not faint.

ISAIAH 40:31, ESV

LORD, I'M LEARNING THAT WAITING IS SURRENDER.

It's not a lesson I'm particularly enjoying, to be perfectly honest. And, apparently, I'm a slow learner because You keep giving me opportunities to practice this lesson.

It seems like I am always waiting.

On the elevator, in the grocery line, in the office, for something big or something small—I don't really want to think about how much time I spend waiting. There's something exhausting about it. Draining. Like an engine stuck in idle, revving and racing and unable to go.

There must be a better way, and I'm quite certain it's Your way. How can I turn these times of waiting into times of renewal, of talking to You?

So that the waiting becomes a time of joy as I soak in Your sustaining presence.

So that the waiting becomes . . . well, worth the wait.

Amen.

When I Lay Me Down to Sleep

In peace I will lie down and sleep,
for you alone, O Lᴏʀᴅ, will keep me safe.

PSALM 4:8

NOW I LAY ME DOWN TO SLEEP . . .

It never fails, Lord. Whenever I do actually lay myself down to rest, the words of that old childhood prayer echo through my mind.

To be honest, though, God, I never really liked that prayer. As a child, it was a bit frightening. But I also remember feeling a touch heathenish whenever I would make up my own words to create a prayer that was more comforting to me.

I've since learned that You welcome my made-up prayers. So . . . please grant me that rest, Lord, as now I lay me down to sleep.

Still the whirling and swirling of my thoughts.

Unknot my muscles, and drain away the tension of the day.

I gather up all my worries, need-to-dos, and didn't-get-dones and place them in Your care.

Surround me. Watch over me and those I love as I rest here—heart and mind, body and soul—trusting in the sacred safety of Your presence with me all through the night.

As now I lay me down to sleep.

Amen.

When It's a Lazy Saturday at Last

The LORD is my shepherd;
I have all that I need.
He lets me rest in green meadows;
he leads me beside peaceful streams.

PSALM 23:1–2

THIS WEEK, LORD . . . this week has been a bit much. A rush-and-crash-through-to-the-end kind of week.

But today is Saturday. *At last.*

No agenda. No real responsibilities. No one demanding my time or attention. (At least not yet.) A day to simply savor, sleep in, and soak up the joy of these nothing-to-do moments.

Lord, I'd so love for this Saturday to be like an empty page waiting to be filled with the things that make me smile . . . or with absolutely nothing at all. And if, by some divine miracle, nothing pops onto my calendar, protect me from feeling like I'm missing out or being left out. Help me remember that I'm a human *being* and not a human *doing* and that it's okay to do nothing sometimes.

May this be a day to move at my own pace or not move much at all. A respite from the wilderness of the rest of the week.

Thank You, God, for the sweet, peace-filled grace of lazy Saturdays.

Amen.

When It's Time to Be Still with God

I wait for the LORD, my whole being waits,
and in his word I put my hope.

PSALM 130:5, NIV

HELP ME STEP INTO YOUR PRESENCE, LORD.

Away from the running and racing of this world.

To be still with You.

Stillness seems like it should be so simple to achieve: *Just stop.* But this world pulls at me, distracting me with everything it says I *should* be doing. It whispers the lie that I don't have time for You. It lures me with ready-to-be-broken promises of "Later . . . later . . . later." But we know how that goes, don't we, God?

Silence the whispers of this world and chase away the distractions. Create in me a thirst for Your presence and a hunger for Your Word. Open my heart, and open my mind. Pour in the light and life of Your truth.

And as I sit here, seeking You, I claim that ancient-yet-unchanging promise: When I seek, You will be found.

Amen.

When It's Easter

Though he was God,
he did not think of equality with God
as something to cling to.
Instead, he gave up his divine privileges;
he took the humble position of a slave
and was born as a human being.

PHILIPPIANS 2:6–7

THE SIGNS OF SPRING ARE ALL AROUND ME, LORD. New blooms and new leaves signal a fresh beginning for the earth.

And because of Jesus, there is a fresh beginning for me.

This new beginning was purchased at an unimaginable cost. Your Son, my Savior, willingly stepped down from all the perfection of heaven and into all the imperfection of this earth. From a rough and wooden manger all the way to a rough and wooden cross, He lived here with us. And He died here for us. For me.

Then, by the might of Your power and the strength of Your love, Lord, You emptied that tomb and offered me a future filled with the wonder and joy of a life lived forever with You.

Who am I, Lord, that You would do all that for me?

Even before my question ends, I hear Your voice whispering the answer: *Who are you? You, dear one, are Mine!*

No simple thank-You could ever be enough. So I give You my life, Lord. Let it be a living praise to You this Easter day and always.

Amen.

When It's Thanksgiving

Always be joyful. Never stop praying.
Be thankful in all circumstances, for this is God's
will for you who belong to Christ Jesus.

1 THESSALONIANS 5:16–18

IT'S THAT SEASON AGAIN, LORD, when it seems that the whole world is taking a moment to be thankful.

Thankful for family and friends.

Thankful for feasts of food.

Thankful for all the different treasures of this world.

And I'm so thankful for all those blessings in my life. But more than any of those things, Lord, I am thankful for You.

You sent Your Son to save me. And if that were all You ever did for me, I would owe You an eternity of everything. But You didn't stop there!

Every day, You choose to step into my life with Your goodness and grace. Sometimes in ways I can see and, other times, in ways that remain a mystery to me. You rescue and redeem, watch over and guide, uphold and sustain—over and over again. Never giving up on me.

So today and every day, I lift up my hands and my song and my praise to You. The One who saved me and keeps right on saving me.

Thank You, Lord, for everything!

Amen.

When It's Christmastime

To us a child is born,
to us a son is given,
and the government will be on his shoulders.
And he will be called
Wonderful Counselor, Mighty God,
Everlasting Father, Prince of Peace.

ISAIAH 9:6, NIV

IT'S CHRISTMASTIME, GOD. One of my favorite times of the year.

The sights, the sounds, the smells—it's as if the air itself sparkles with hope and joy and possibility.

As I think about all the gifts I want to gather and give—and, yes, even one or two I might like to receive—I can't help but also think about Your Gift to me.

A Gift of love, of mercy and grace, of salvation. All wrapped in the most unlikely of packages. Tucked away for only a carpenter and his wife, a few shepherds, and a handful of animals to see.

A Gift that You planned before the beginning and knew I would desperately need.

Jesus.

Immanuel.

God with us.

Lord, I praise You for being God with me.

Amen.

PRAYERS
FOR ON
THE GO

When I'm So Busy

Jesus replied: " 'Love the Lord your God
with all your heart and with all your soul
and with all your mind.' This is the first and
greatest commandment. And the second
is like it: 'Love your neighbor as yourself.' "

MATTHEW 22:37–39, NIV

I'M SO BUSY, LORD!

I wonder how many times each day You hear those words. Too many times, I'm sure, just from me.

I've got commitments, obligations, and opportunities . . .

There. Is. So. Much.

I can't get all these things done. The list is too long. Tasks and chores and endless emails. The printer refuses to print, and that "I'm processing" symbol keeps popping up on my computer screen like a crazed, rainbow-colored spinning wheel of doom. The phone is ringing, texts are pinging, and I am panicking.

Help!

Clear away the clutter of this day. Show me this busyness as You see it. Teach me what is important and what isn't.

Help me remember that if I do the two most important things—love others and love You—then this day counts as a win. No matter what does or doesn't get done.

Amen.

When I'm Facing the Same Task for the Thousandth Time

God is able to bless you abundantly, so that
in all things at all times, having all that you need,
you will abound in every good work.

2 CORINTHIANS 9:8, NIV

LORD, I'M LOOKING AROUND AND WONDERING, *Who's going to take care of this?* And I'm realizing it's me. *It's still me.*

It's been me for the last 999 times this needed doing. Ten years from now, it will be me. Even when I'm on my deathbed, I'll probably have to get up and take care of this because it's *still going to be me.*

It's not that this chore is particularly huge or hard. I'm just tired of doing it.

Ugh. I'm whining again, aren't I? I'm sorry. (But You did listen to the Israelites in the desert for all those years, so perhaps You don't mind too much . . . ? Okay, You're right. That probably isn't the best example.)

Maybe I need to think of this a different way. How do *You* see this chore? Could it become something I *get* to do instead of *have* to do? Or could I do it mindlessly, without thinking about it, so that it actually makes room to spend time with You?

How can I turn this never-ending task into a time of worship?

As I fold these clothes, mow this lawn, or clear out this inbox—as I do this same task for the 3,376th time—show me how to do it for You. Show me the blessings behind and within this endless chore.

And thank You for putting up with whiners like me.

Amen.

When I Am Interrupted

Let your gentleness be evident to all.
The Lord is near.

PHILIPPIANS 4:5, NIV

LORD, I HAVE SO MUCH TO GET DONE TODAY. The list is long, and the hours are flying by. Yet the interruptions are endless and unrelenting. I can feel my patience stretching thin and my words turning sharp.

This is not who I want to be.

I don't want to be hurried or harsh.

I don't want to be bound or defined by the items I accomplish.

I don't want to miss what truly matters because I've allowed myself to be led by a list.

What I do want, Lord, is to be patient and kind.

I want to be bound and defined by Your love and generosity.

I want to live out a day filled with moments that matter.

Sift through my heart and order my priorities. Toss away any selfishness. And give me the wisdom to discern which interruptions I should ignore and which are divine appointments set by You.

Amen.

When I Finally Get a Little Win

Because you are my help,
I sing in the shadow of your wings.

PSALM 63:7, NIV

YOU KNOW, GOD, there's a lot of ordinary (maybe even less-than-ordinary) that seems to fill up so much of my days. Maybe that's why this win feels so *amazing*!

In the grand scheme of things, I know it's not huge. There won't be any red-carpet awards or picture-snapping paparazzi. (Though *I* might snap a selfie or two!) But *we* know that this one goes in the win column, don't we, God?

That's enough to keep me going.

Not trudging along but diving into this day—amid all the ordinary and mundane—with a smile on my face and joy in my heart.

Because I also know that this win is a gift. You saw that I needed a little encouragement, a reason to celebrate, and a reminder that You are right here beside me in even the most mundane. So You picked out this gift of a win just for me.

And, God? It fits perfectly!

Amen.

When Five O'Clock on Friday
Seems Like It Will Never Come

In all the work you are doing,
work the best you can.
Work as if you were doing it for
the Lord, not for people.

COLOSSIANS 3:23, NCV

LORD, IT SHOULD BE FIVE O'CLOCK. It really should. It's been at least eleventy-seven hours since morning, and it should be time to end this day. But it's not.

I know. I've been watching the clock. I'm tempted to get up and check its batteries because the hands don't seem to be moving at all. But the time it tells agrees perfectly with the clock on my computer and the clock on my phone (which I've also been watching).

I'm grateful for this work, Lord. I really am. It's just that right now I want to be *not* here at this job. I want to be out the door with my shoes pointed toward home. I want to be on my couch with my comfy clothes on. I want to be where the only demands placed on me are my own.

I don't mean to wish time away or waste one minute of it. But, Lord, could You please help it be five o'clock very, very soon?

Amen.

When I'm Stuck in Traffic

Be joyful in hope, patient in affliction, faithful in prayer.

ROMANS 12:12, NIV

DEAR LORD, CARS AND ROADS were made for going, but we're not going. *At all.*

My frustration level is ratcheting up. I realize I'm getting far too upset over something I can't do anything about. The temptation to lash out is so . . . well, *tempting.*

Calm my spirit.

Open my eyes to see and my heart to remember that everyone around me is Your beloved creation. Yes, even that person riding my bumper and that guy uselessly honking his horn. (I mean, does he not understand that I would go if I could? Sorry, God. Taking another deep breath now.)

Guide us all safely through this tangled mess to where we each need to be.

And since I'm stuck here, change my thinking so that I see this as an opportunity.

To lift up those around me in prayer.

To consider the wonders of Your creation that I would otherwise be zooming right past.

To spend time with You.

Amen.

When I Am Plagued by Distractions

We capture every thought and
make it give up and obey Christ.

2 CORINTHIANS 10:5, NCV

GOD, I DESPERATELY NEED TO FOCUS my thoughts and efforts on this task in front of me. The deadlines are real, and the consequences of procrastinating are not good.

But a thousand little "squirrels" are dashing through my brain right now, distracting me and pulling me in a million different directions.

As soon as I rein in one wandering thought, two more scurry in to take its place. From puzzling over what to do about dinner (I should google new recipes) to wondering if people ever really thought the moon was made of cheese (I could look that up too), I feel as if I've run a marathon just chasing down my thoughts.

Capture my thoughts, Lord.

They're not listening to me, so please make them give up and obey You. Focus my thoughts so that I can do what needs to be done.

Amen.

When Technology Isn't Cooperating

Do not be anxious about anything, but in every
situation, by prayer and petition, with
thanksgiving, present your requests to God.

PHILIPPIANS 4:6, NIV

LORD, EVERY INCH, EVERY MOLECULE of this universe is Your creation. You
understand it all, and You are able to control it all. From the waves of the sea and
the phases of the moon all the way down to this technological mess I am facing.

In the back of my mind, a thought is whispering that this prayer is silly and that I
shouldn't be bothering You. But You encourage me to bring all my troubles and all
my requests to You.

So here I am.

Because my panic is rising and my blood pressure is soaring, and I fear that so much
of what I've worked on is about to disappear into electronic oblivion.

I ask You, Lord—the One who is over all and in all—to rearrange all these bits
and bytes so that they talk to each other and play nice with each other. Tame this
technological beast, and make it do what it was created to do.

Please.

And thank You.

And amen.

When I'm Traveling

The LORD himself will go before you.
He will be with you; he will not leave you or
forget you. Don't be afraid and don't worry.

DEUTERONOMY 31:8, NCV

IT'S TRAVELING TIME AGAIN, GOD. Off to see the world . . . or at least a little corner of it.

Go before me and clear the paths. You know that I don't mind a little boring when it comes to the mechanics of cars and trains and planes. Keep my travels safe, with no accidents or incidents.

Guide me to the places You would have me go, to the things You would have me see, and to the experiences You have planned for me. Open my eyes and my heart to the people You want me to meet.

And wherever I go—across town, across the country, or across the world—remind me that I never really travel alone. You are before and behind and all around me. There's not a single step or breath that I take without You by my side.

Thank You for that, God.

Amen.

When My Thoughts Won't Stop Spinning

[Jesus] awoke and rebuked the wind and
said to the sea, "Peace! Be still!" And the wind
ceased, and there was a great calm.

MARK 4:39, ESV

I CANNOT REST, FATHER.

I cannot seem to settle.

I desperately need my thoughts to be still, but they refuse. Instead, they swirl around and around in my mind like a whirlwind, completely out of control.

Thoughts of *worries* and *work* and *what to do* crash together like waves against the rocks, breaking up and shattering my peace.

I can't seem to stop this storm inside me. But You can.

You can still any storm.

Whether it's a storm on the waters or a storm of thoughts inside my mind.

Still my thoughts, Lord.

Still this storm as You speak words of peace over me. And lead me to the safe harbor of rest in You.

Amen.

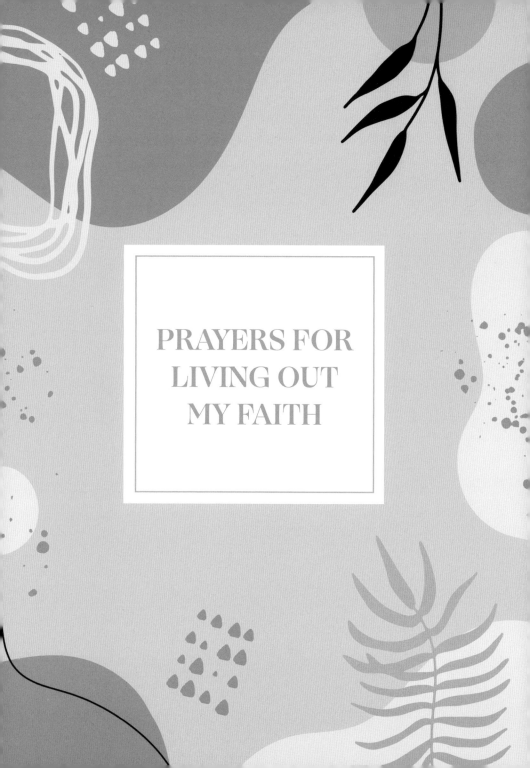

PRAYERS FOR
LIVING OUT
MY FAITH

When I Try to Live a Life of Faith

Don't be afraid, for I am with you.
Don't be discouraged, for I am your God.
I will strengthen you and help you.
I will hold you up with my victorious right hand.

ISAIAH 41:10

I WANT TO LIVE A LIFE OF FAITH, GOD.

I want to do all the things that would cause You to look at me and say, "Well done, good and faithful one."

But it isn't easy. It's a battle each and every day. Often it feels like the world is throwing everything it has at me, and it's all I can do to stay standing. And then there are the battles raging within me—battles against selfishness, vanity, and pride.

I'm beaten up and battle-scarred. But I'm not defeated.

Because You are not defeated. You won the victory on that cross two thousand years ago. The devil just can't seem to admit it.

Help me keep fighting this fight. To keep battling with truth and love and light to show the world who You are and how much You love them.

And thank You for always being faithful to help me live out my faith.

Amen.

When I'm Welcoming Others into My Home

The Lord said to her, "My dear Martha,
you are worried and upset over all these details!
There is only one thing worth being concerned
about. Mary has discovered it, and it will not
be taken away from her."

LUKE 10:41–42

I'M THINKING OF CHANGING MY NAME, LORD.

I'm thinking of calling myself Martha, because that's who I feel like right now. I'm rushing and hurrying and worrying over all the details: the food, the dishes, the dog . . . the baseboards! (Does anyone even notice baseboards?)

There *are* things that need to be done, but help me remember that they don't have to be done to perfection. No magazine crew is coming to take photos. No one will be taking notes or documenting all I haven't done.

Remind me of what matters most. The greatest part of any gathering is how welcomed and wanted my guests feel.

Relax the knots of tension, and help me smile from the inside out, so that I can welcome each guest into my heart and home . . . just as You welcome me into Yours.

Amen.

When I Need to Let Go

If any of you wants to be my follower, you must
give up your own way, take up your cross daily,
and follow me.

LUKE 9:23

GOD, I'VE BEEN HOLDING ON SO TIGHTLY.

I've been trying to control and force everything into place . . . the way *I* think it should be.

The results are not good. In fact, they're pretty disastrous. I told myself that I could handle all this and that I didn't need to bother You. I was so very wrong. Forgive my arrogance and stubborn pride. Any sense of control I had was only a laughable illusion.

Even knowing that, though, it's still ridiculously hard for me to loosen my grip and let go. Help me lay all my concerns in Your hands, surrender them to Your care, and trust You to take control.

Your will. Not mine.

And, God? Please keep working on me until my whole life is a reflection of those words:

Your will. Not mine.

Amen.

When I Am Tempted to Judge

When he saw the crowds, he had compassion
on them, because they were harassed and
helpless, like sheep without a shepherd.

MATTHEW 9:36, NIV

HERE I AM AGAIN, GOD, asking You to forgive me.

What for this time? Trying to steal Your job. Your *judging* job.

I saw this person. The way they dressed. The things they did and said. And I jumped straight to a conclusion about who they were.

Then I learned that I know nothing at all.

They're not like I thought, God. And the reasons behind their words and actions? Well, there but for Your mercy and grace go I.

How many times have I done this? How many times will I make this same mistake?

I'm so sorry. You offer Your grace and goodness and truth—Your compassion—to everyone. And so should I.

Thank You for giving *me* grace, even though I've messed up yet again. And thank You for not dismissing me as a lost cause.

Amen.

When I Should Say No

If you go the wrong way—to the right or to the
left—you will hear a voice behind you saying,
"This is the right way. You should go this way."

ISAIAH 30:21, NCV

LORD, I NEED TO SAY NO.

Right?

This really is a good thing I've been asked to do. It would bring joy to others, and it would serve You. And, honestly, the praise I would get for doing it would feel awfully good.

I'm just not quite sure how I can make it happen along with everything else I've promised to do.

If I say yes to this, then I'll have to say no to something else. Which, realistically, right now, means saying no to those closest to me. Because they'll still be around when this is done. (At least that's what I tell myself.) Or it means saying no to taking care of myself—and yes to dinners on the run, late nights, and even rushed-through moments with You.

What do You think, God?

This isn't for me, is it? At least not right now.

So please help me find the courage to say, "Thank you, but I need to say no."

Amen.

When I Need to Say Yes

Let's not get tired of doing what is good.
At just the right time we will reap a harvest
of blessing if we don't give up.

GALATIANS 6:9

LORD, I CAN THINK OF A MILLION REASONS—or at least half a dozen really good ones—to say no to this request.

When would I have time? Look at all that would need to be done! How can I say yes when I'm already stretched more than a little thin?

Still, my heart keeps telling me that I need to say yes.

The verses running on repeat through my thoughts are telling me to say yes.

These nudges I feel from You in my heart are telling me to say yes.

Okay, Lord, I'm going to say yes. I'm stepping out on this limb of obedience and trusting that You won't let me fall.

As for all the hows, whats, and whens—well, I'm trusting You to work those out too.

Amen.

When I Need to Hear God's Voice

After the earthquake a fire, but the LORD was not
in the fire; and after the fire a still small voice.

1 KINGS 19:12, NKJV

FATHER?

I need to hear Your voice.

I need the comfort of Your presence.

I need the guidance and reassurance of Your Word.

The world around me is roaring and loud, and it's devouring all my attempts to find Your peace.

Overcome the world. Once more. For me. In this moment.

Hush the noise around me. Quiet the thunder of my own wayward and rambling thoughts. Silence everything. Everything but Your still, small voice.

I'm listening, Lord. I am trying so hard to listen.

Help me not miss one single word.

Amen.

When Temptation Comes Knocking

Don't let us yield to temptation,
but rescue us from the evil one.

MATTHEW 6:13

I AM SO TEMPTED, LORD.

I am tempted to do what I know I shouldn't do, the very thing I *promised* I wouldn't do.

And yet . . .

It would be easy. Wickedness whispers that it isn't so very wrong. It would feel so good to give in. And there are the age-old excuses: *Everyone is doing it. Who would ever know? Whom would it really hurt?*

Yes, You're right. It would hurt.

It would hurt me, and it would hurt You.

It would hurt the relationship between us.

Those "feel good" feelings would vanish all too quickly, and then the guilt and shame would pour in.

Please give me the strength to turn away and not give in. Change my will and my wants until they match Yours.

When temptation comes knocking, Lord, help me bolt the door.

Amen.

When I Use the Gift God's Given Me

God has given each of you a gift
from his great variety of spiritual gifts.
Use them well to serve one another.

1 PETER 4:10

THIS ABILITY I HAVE, LORD? I know it's from You. I'm just not always quite sure what to do with it.

I want to be faithful with this gift You've given me and use it for good and Your glory. I don't want to waste it or leave it sitting on the shelf.

I've been given a chance to step out and use my gift. I believe it's a path You want me to follow—and in a burst of beautifully divine coincidence, it's what I want too. You know I could race down this path like lightning. But I don't ever want to race ahead of You and Your plans for me.

If this isn't a path I should follow or if I should use my gift another way, make that clear and lead me to the path You've laid out for me. Because I don't want to do anything that isn't blessed by You.

But if this does happen to be Your will? Well, I wouldn't mind that one bit!

And, God? Thank You for this gift.

Amen.

When Something Unexpected Happens

You saw me before I was born.
Every day of my life was recorded in your book.
Every moment was laid out
before a single day had passed.

PSALM 139:16

WELL, I WASN'T EXPECTING *that,* God.

I thought perhaps this might happen or even this instead. But *that?* I didn't see it coming at all. And I'm not sure what to think or do—or even how to feel.

Which is why I'm here.

None of this is a surprise to You. You saw it coming before it ever began. You've got a plan in place to get me through, and You'll give me everything I need to handle this in a way that honors You.

I believe that, God. I really do.

But . . . I'd be ever so grateful if You would let me in on that plan or at least the next step in it. Because this has caught me completely off guard. I need Your wisdom and peace right now.

Wrap Your arms around me, and hold me close. Just for a little while. Whisper that everything will be okay. Somehow. Someway.

I know that nothing comes to me—whether good or evil—unless it first goes through You.

Show me how to be Your light on this unexpected path.

Amen.

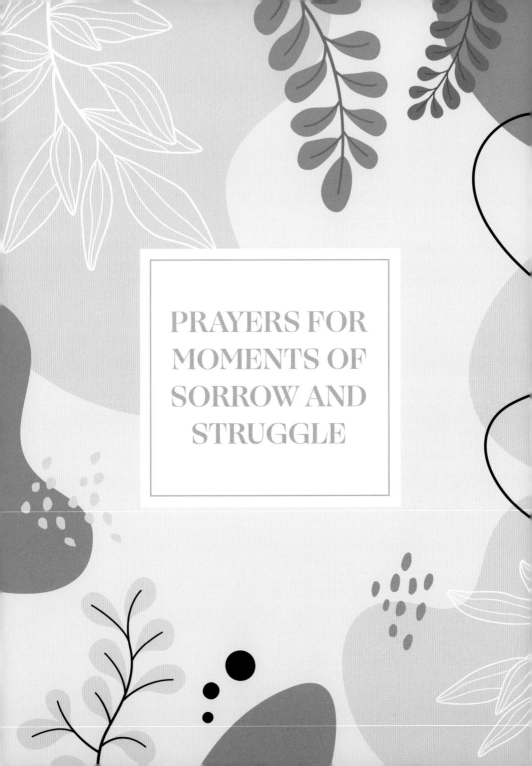

PRAYERS FOR MOMENTS OF SORROW AND STRUGGLE

When I Need God to Reign

The Lord reigns as king forever.
The Lord gives his people strength.
The Lord blesses them with peace.

PSALM 29:10–11

LORD, THIS WORLD HAS GONE CRAZY. It's become frightening. For me. For those I love. For Your people everywhere.

There are earthquakes and fires and storms. There are wars and rumors of wars. Both literal and figurative. It feels like complete chaos is coming. There's nothing I alone can do. It's all so far beyond my control.

But it's not beyond Your control.

So I come to You now, and I ask You—beg You—to reign.

Reign, Lord!

Reign in my heart.

Reign in my home.

Reign in this world.

Let every person and every heart see the wonder, the power, and the might of who You are.

Please, Lord. *Reign.*

Amen.

When I Need to Do a Hard Thing

I can do all things through Christ,
because he gives me strength.

PHILIPPIANS 4:13, NCV

THERE'S SOMETHING I NEED TO DO, GOD.

It won't be easy. In fact, it's going to be hard. Almost impossibly hard.

Almost.

I'm scared. It would be so much easier to duck and run and disappear. But I need to show up in this moment. I can't take the easy way out. I can't pretend this problem doesn't exist or isn't mine to handle.

I need to do this hard thing.

I need Your strength to do it.

And I know You'll be with me every step of the way, helping me do what needs to be done.

Thank You for being the God I can count on. Always.

Amen.

When I Am Not Feeling My Best

Heal me, Lᴏʀᴅ, and I will be healed;
save me and I will be saved,
for you are the one I praise.

JEREMIAH 17:14, NIV

GOD, I'M NOT FEELING MY BEST TODAY. Actually, I'm not feeling well at all.

There's nothing I can really do about it. Except be still and rest. And we both know how good I am at that. This inability to go and do and get things done is making me a little crazy. I feel stuck. Used up and useless.

It's silly to think, *I can't be sick* or *I don't have time for this.*

As if I'm letting the world down by taking time to rest.

After all, *You* are still in control.

Soothe away the aches, the guilts, and all the I-should-be-doings.

Please be the Great Physician and nurture my body so that it can work the way You designed it to.

And not just for me, God. So many others battle illnesses much worse than an interruption or an inconvenience. Stay close beside them. Hold and heal them.

Just as I trust You to hold and heal me.

Amen.

When I'm Awake in the Night

Speak, LORD. I am your servant and I am listening.

1 SAMUEL 3:10, NCV

WELL, HERE WE ARE AGAIN, LORD. It's far too late—or perhaps far too early—for me to be awake.

I should be sleeping. I *need* to be sleeping. *Unless* . . . was that Your still, small voice that awakened me?

Open my heart to listen.

In this dark and sleepy sleepless space, fill my mind with Your voice. Let Your words of comfort and promise whisper to me. Guide me to what You would have me hear, learn, and do.

Or could it be that there is someone, Lord, who needs my care and attention?

Someone who needs me to lift them up to You?

You are surely here with me in the stillness of this night. I curl up in Your arms like a child, breathing deeply and slowly in Your holy presence.

Listening, leaning in, settling in . . . and trusting always in You.

Amen.

When God Feels Far Away

Come near to God and he will come near to you.

JAMES 4:8, NIV

YOU ARE HERE WITH ME, GOD—right where You've promised to be. I believe that. I really do.

But I'm not feeling Your presence.

It's as if You're a million miles away from me. Though, I guess, the truth is probably that *I* am a million miles away from You.

Have I become too busy? Am I too caught up in myself? Or have I strayed from Your path? Show me what's creating this distance between us.

Forgive me.

Come for me, Father. Draw me back to You.

Amen.

When I Need God to Show Off

Nothing will be impossible with God.

LUKE 1:37, ESV

HOLY FATHER, I NEED YOU to show off in this moment and in this situation.

I can do nothing, but there's nothing You can't do. You have the power, the might, and the wisdom to make everything all right—better than all right.

I'm not asking You to show *up,* because You are already here and already working. But I am boldly asking You to show *off* in the way You work this out. Not just for me. (Though I won't deny that I would love to see it!) But for all those who will see— who *need* to see—Your love and power at work.

Be big!

Be bold!

Be undeniable!

Let there be no doubt that You are at work in this.

Show off, Father. Your will. Your way. And all to Your glory.

Amen.

When I'm Exhausted

Jesus said, "Come to me, all of you who are weary
and carry heavy burdens, and I will give you rest."

MATTHEW 11:28

I AM SO TIRED, LORD.

I feel as if I run and run all day and accomplish nothing. I'm chasing after the wind, like Solomon said, and I'm exhausted because I can't catch it.

Night comes, and I crash into my pillow. Even my dreams are filled with the same rush and hurry of my days. When morning arrives, the whirlwind picks up and begins all over again.

I need a nap. I need a vacation. I need . . . *You.*

Quiet the chaos, Lord.

I kneel here in this moment of prayer. This moment that's just You and me. I close my eyes and lean my head against Your knee. I can almost feel Your hand upon me as You whisper, *I will give you the rest you need.*

My heart slows, and my mind clears. Whether it's been a moment, a minute, or an hour, I am refreshed here in Your presence. In this moment that's just You and me.

Amen.

When I'm Struggling to Believe

I do believe; help me overcome my unbelief!

MARK 9:24, NIV

LORD, YOU ARE GOOD, You are God, and You are in control. Right now, though, I'm struggling to see that goodness and control.

People come to me with questions about You and about my faith that I'm not sure how to answer. I even have a few questions of my own. There's so much I don't understand.

When I read through the psalms, I see that David and the other writers pretty much threw everything at You—all their doubts, questions, and fears. Even their anger.

You listened. And You led them back to trusting, believing, and praising You.

So I'm laying everything I'm thinking and feeling and wondering here before You.

I *do* believe You are listening.

I *do* believe that You hear and You care.

Lead me through these moments when I struggle to believe—through these doubts, questions, and fears. Lead me to trust You more than I ever have before.

Amen.

When I Feel Attacked

The Lord himself will fight for you. Just stay calm.

EXODUS 14:14

HOLY FATHER, I FEEL as if I'm under attack.

Not by any one person or group. At least, not that I can see or call by name. It's as if my life is filling up with sorrows and fears and shadows. Like there's an unseen, invisible enemy determined to defeat me and make me doubt You.

You tell me that the real battles of this world are against the powers of evil and darkness. Honestly, that terrifies me. But You promise not only that You will fight for me but also that You've already defeated this enemy. That You are greater than anyone or anything who would come against me.

So I choose to trust in You.

Keep me close to You. Shield me and fight for me. Chase away the darkness, the shadows, and the fear. Shine Your light so bright in and through my life that everyone around me sees You.

And help me, Lord, to hold on for Your victory.

Amen.

When I Need God to Make a Way

See, I am doing a new thing!
Now it springs up; do you not perceive it?
I am making a way in the wilderness
and streams in the wasteland.

ISAIAH 43:19, NIV

GOD, I DON'T SEE THE ANSWER. I don't see the way. But You do.

You know the best answer and the perfect path to take.

It's so tempting to rush to the end, to the answer—to *any* answer that might make this all go away. Help me, instead, to hold fast to Your hand and walk with You.

Nothing is impossible for You, and I trust that right at this very moment You are already working to make a way through this wilderness. You're creating an answer so big, so beautiful, and so perfect, it could only come from You.

Your love is so great that You are willing to reach down and rescue, to make a way for me. You've done it before, and I know You'll do it again.

So I will wait.

I will trust.

And when Your answer comes, I will walk out of this wilderness with You.

Amen.

PRAYERS
OF WINS,
WORRIES, AND
BLESSINGS

When It's Been an Amazing Day

Rejoice in the Lord always. I will say it again: Rejoice!

PHILIPPIANS 4:4, NIV

ABBA, IT HAS BEEN THE BEST. DAY. EVER.

Well, at least in the top ten. So far.

From the moment I got out of bed, everything seemed to fall into place. It was even a great hair day!

It felt not only like everything was turning out just right but also like I was making a difference. Like what I was doing mattered. And I think it's because I felt so in sync with You and what You wanted me to do.

I know You're always right by my side, working in my life. I *know* that. But today I *felt* it. I *felt* Your presence. And it was a glimpse of how it will be one day when I fully live with You.

So, yes, I'm loving everything that went so well and right in my day. But most of all, I'm loving being this close to You.

Thank You, God, for spending the day with me. You made it amazing!

Amen.

When I'm Celebrating the Impossible

O Sovereign LORD! You made the heavens
and earth by your strong hand and powerful
arm. Nothing is too hard for you!

JEREMIAH 32:17

GOD, I DIDN'T THINK IT COULD BE DONE. And I definitely didn't think I could do it. Well, I suppose I got that last part right.

I didn't do it.

You did!

Because nothing is impossible for You.

The odds were against me right from the start. But I prayed hard and worked hard, and I trusted You to work it out the way You wanted to.

And I'm *really* glad this is the way You wanted it all to go! You are so, so good to me.

But, God, I do want to remind myself of this truth: Even if I didn't do it—even if I flopped and failed and face-planted in front of the whole world—You would still be good. I would still trust in You.

And that's always a reason to celebrate.

Amen.

When I Need to Celebrate
Someone Else's Win

"I know the plans I have for you," says the LORD.
"They are plans for good and not for
disaster, to give you a future and a hope."

JEREMIAH 29:11

FATHER, I GUESS THIS IS THE TIME to confess that I'm not quite who I want to be. Not quite who You want me to be.

I didn't get what I wanted—what I hoped and worked for. Someone else did. And, honestly, they deserved it. I can see how this will be awesome for them and how they will be awesome in this opportunity.

Help me as I try to hide my disappointment. I want to rejoice and celebrate with my friend. I want to help them succeed in any way I can.

But I need You to banish this little bit of jealousy that's lingering here in my heart. I trust and believe that You are already at work to bring Your blessings to life in my life. In a way that will fit perfectly in Your plan for me.

Help me celebrate with my friend as I wait to see what You do.

Amen.

When I Am Anxious

Cast all your anxiety on him because he cares for you.

1 PETER 5:7, NIV

LORD, YOU INVITE ME to cast my cares, my worries, my fears, and my anxieties on You. Actually, Your words read more like a command: Cast your cares.

So here I am, Lord. Rod in hand. Reel at the ready. Casting. And hoping to hook the peace of Your presence.

The thing is, it's difficult to name these anxieties, these whispering fears that make my heart beat a little too fast and steal my peace, my focus, and my slumber.

It's as if there's a hum and thrum of . . . of . . . *unsettledness* vibrating through me. Keeping my muscles tense and my nerves on edge. Keeping me just a little worried about the world, this day, and tomorrow. About anything and everything and nothing much at all.

And this hum and thrum drowns out what I most want to fill my thoughts and my days with: the love and joy and presence of those You've given me. The love and joy of Your presence.

There is so much that I do not and cannot know in this world—and that's probably for the best. But this I do know:

You are God.

You are good.

You are in control.

And I will trust You to care for me now and to take care of my anxieties.

Amen.

When I'm Trapped in Comparisons

We are God's masterpiece. He has created
us anew in Christ Jesus, so we can do the
good things he planned for us long ago.

EPHESIANS 2:10

GOD, AS I LOOK AT THE WORLD around me—at what others are doing and achieving—I feel like I don't measure up. Like I'm somehow *less than* and *not enough*.

Even when I do succeed at something (at least as the world defines *succeed*), I find myself feeling like an impostor, waiting to be found out for the fraud I really am.

But as these thoughts ricochet around my mind, I also hear a snippet of a verse whispering to me, telling me that I should listen not to the world but to You.

Because You don't measure success by counting awards or accolades. You measure success in increments of love.

Help me hear *Your* voice. Drown out the doubts and fears. Saturate my heart with reminders of who I really am and who I can encourage others to be . . .

Yours.

Fearfully and wonderfully made. On purpose and for a purpose. A masterpiece handcrafted by the One who scooped out oceans and scattered stars.

Never let me forget, Lord, that I am Yours. And that's enough for me.

Amen.

When I Worry I'm Not Doing Enough

What can I offer the LORD
for all he has done for me?
I will lift up the cup of salvation
and praise the LORD's name for saving me.

PSALM 116:12-13

LORD, I SEE SO MANY NEEDS all around me. Needs that are far too many for me to meet and far greater than I can handle.

I try to help when and where I can here in my own little corner of the world. But I'm worried that it isn't enough.

You've given me so much, Abba. So much love, so much grace, and so many blessings.

I want to give back.

I realize I can never give back enough to repay all You've done for me. That's the wonder of this whole relationship between me and You. Still, I want to be found trying.

Not to earn Your blessings but to praise You for them and help others find them in You.

So please accept these things I do as my humble gift to You. Multiply my efforts, and make them enough in the way that only You can. And if I can do more, show me that too.

Amen.

When I Didn't Completely Mess It Up

I lift up my eyes to the mountains—
where does my help come from?
My help comes from the LORD,
the Maker of heaven and earth.

PSALM 121:1–2, NIV

I WAS SURE THAT I WOULD, LORD. I was convinced that I would completely mess up this opportunity.

But I didn't. In fact, I think it actually went pretty well.

And, honestly, I don't think that had much to do with me.

Because I've been doing this whole life thing long enough to know that my personal ability to mess things up is quite vast. Practically legendary.

Which is why I didn't rely on myself. I chose to rely on You instead. (Good thing, huh?)

I covered every moment, every step, and every possible misstep in prayer. And You leaned down from heaven and listened. Just as You always do.

You built up the hedges of protection around me. You smoothed out the path before me and cleared away the obstacles that would have tripped me up. You filled my mind with Your wisdom, my heart with Your love, and my mouth with Your words.

And because of You, I didn't mess up.

Thank You, God. So very much.

Amen.

When I Feel Helpless

The Lord is my strength and my shield;
my heart trusts in him, and he helps me.

PSALM 28:7, NIV

LORD, I DON'T KNOW WHAT TO DO. I've tried everything I can think of, and this situation isn't getting any better. This is just too big for me. And I'm feeling completely . . . *helpless.*

Even as I speak those words, I realize what I'm saying. I've tried to do it all on my own again, haven't I?

I've tried to do it without You.

Forgive me, God. I guess I was in such a hurry to step in and make everything all right that I didn't stop to ask You to go before me and guide me. I need You in this situation, in every situation, and for every step I take.

So can I please try again?

Take control, Lord.

Of this situation.

Of my actions and reactions.

Of the outcome.

I may be helpless, but You are always the help I need.

Amen.

When I'm Looking
for the Plan and Purpose

We know that God causes everything
to work together for the good of
those who love God and are called
according to his purpose for them.

ROMANS 8:28

LORD, I BELIEVE YOU HAVE A PLAN and a purpose for this day. I believe You have a place just for me within that plan and purpose. And I believe You're already here in this moment, busy and working to put it all into place.

How can I join You, Lord, in this sacred work You are doing today?

Help me remember that Your work might not look like a grand and glorious mission. It might not look like anything sacred at all. In fact, it might look a lot more like tackling weekend chores or handling the endless needs of those around me. It might look like navigating traffic, punching a time clock, or ducking and dodging watercooler politics—all while still trying to show the world Your goodness and grace.

After all, it's not what I do. Not really. It's Your presence and purpose that transform my efforts into sacred work.

So, Lord, how can I work together with You today?

Amen.

When I'm Glad to Be Me

I praise you because I am fearfully and wonderfully made;
your works are wonderful,
I know that full well.

PSALM 139:14, NIV

I'LL ADMIT, LORD, THAT THERE ARE DAYS when I listen to others and to the world instead of You. And I begin to believe the lie that maybe I'm not quite *enough* somehow.

But today is *not* one of those days.

Am I a little different? Definitely!

Am I a little quirky? Quite quirky sometimes.

Am I even a little weird? Occasionally, but in a weirdly awesome sort of way.

In fact, the more birthdays I get under my belt, the more I'm learning to not only like but also *enjoy* who You created me to be.

Sure, I'm still a work in progress—and there are times when that workload is a lot! But the more I learn about myself and where I fit in Your kingdom and in Your plan, the more I realize that there isn't anyone else I'd rather be. There are things I can do and ways I can do those things that no one else can.

So thank You, God. I'm so glad You made me . . . *me!*

Amen.

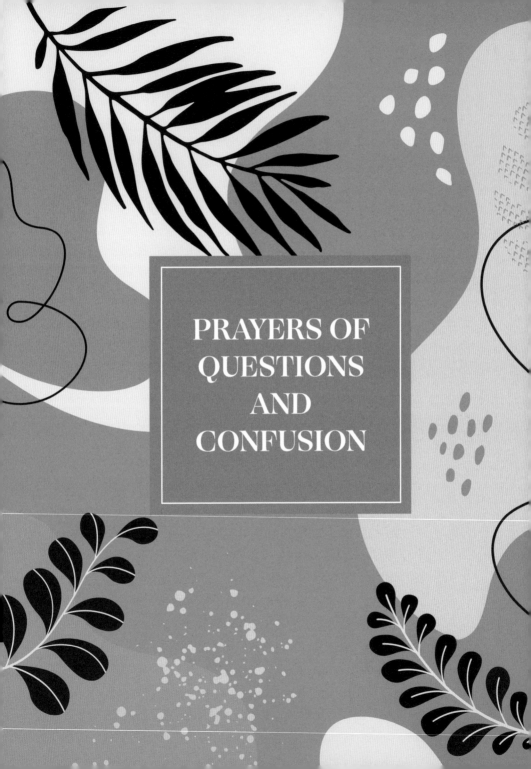

PRAYERS OF QUESTIONS AND CONFUSION

When I Don't Know What to Pray

We do not know how to pray as we should.
But the Spirit himself speaks to God
for us, even begs God for us with deep
feelings that words cannot explain.

ROMANS 8:26, NCV

LORD, I DON'T KNOW WHAT TO PRAY. I don't know what to ask or even hope for.

So I'm doing what I hope I'll always do when I don't know what to do. I'm coming to You.

Could I just sit here with You?

Could I let my mind and heart rest?

Could I just *be* for a little while?

No striving, no trying, no working hard to figure it all out. Instead, I'll let Your Spirit intercede and speak for me.

And I'll listen for Your answers.

As we sit here together.

You and me.

Amen.

When a Prayer Isn't Answered

I will answer them before they even call to me.
While they are still talking about their needs,
I will go ahead and answer their prayers!

ISAIAH 65:24

I'M AT A LOSS, LORD.

You didn't answer my prayer. I've waited and prayed and waited . . . and still, there is no response. Only Your silence.

I *need* to hear from You. Why aren't You answering, Abba?

. . . Oh.

I think maybe I'm beginning to understand.

You *are* answering. You have been right from the start, haven't You? It just isn't the answer I was hoping for.

Is it "No" forever? Or is it "No, not right now"?

I'll keep praying and listening and trusting You. Because I know You hear every prayer. You respond to every request I lift up with an invitation into conversation. So help me draw close and listen for Your answers to my prayers.

Amen.

When the Future Feels So Uncertain

The LORD is in his holy Temple;
the LORD still rules from heaven.

PSALM 11:4

IT'S A GREAT BIG SCARY WORLD out there, God. And my own life is feeling pretty uncertain too.

I don't know what's going to happen. Not today or tomorrow or next year.

But You do.

You're writing this story. From the very beginning to the ultimate end—including every word, page, and chapter in between. And while I may not know all the hows or whats or what-will-happen-nexts, I do know the ending. Because You've told me. More than that, You've *promised* me. This story—my story—ends in a happily ever after with You.

It's still a great big scary world out there. But I'm not in it alone. Not for a moment. And Your presence gives me the courage to step out—and even dare to smile—amid all the unknowns.

Amen.

When I Feel Invisible

She gave this name to the L*ord* who spoke to her:
"You are the God who sees me," for she said,
"I have now seen the One who sees me."

GENESIS 16:13, NIV

IT'S NOT THAT I WANT to be center stage, Lord.

I'm not looking to be a star. But . . .

It would be nice to be noticed.

To be invited into the circle instead of standing outside.

To be seen once in a while.

I could really use one of Your reminders now, Lord. Those reminders that I'm not invisible to You, *El Roi,* the God who sees me. Reminders like these:

> *You created me. You knit me together stitch by stitch and cell by cell, weaving Your image into my mind and body, heart and soul.*
>
> *You sing over me and delight in me.*
>
> *You call me Your own.*
>
> *You invite me into Your presence, and I am never outside Your notice or care.*
>
> *I am never invisible to You.*

Thank You, Father, for seeing—and for reminding—me.

Amen.

When I Don't Understand

Trust in the Lᴏʀᴅ with all your heart;
do not depend on your own understanding.
Seek his will in all you do,
and he will show you which path to take.

PROVERBS 3:5–6

GOD, I DON'T UNDERSTAND.

This isn't the way I was hoping things would go. It isn't the path I would have chosen to take. I placed this whole situation in Your hands and in Your care . . . and here we are. In a place I don't understand and don't particularly want to be.

I'm hurt, I'm frustrated, and I'm angry. I'm tempted to rage a little and maybe even rebel.

But . . .

I remember Your promises and that Your plans are for my good—not to harm or hurt me.

I remember all the ways You have walked with me in the past, rescued me, lifted me up, and sustained me.

I remember that I am Your child, dearly loved by You. The child You sacrificed Your own Son to save.

No, I don't understand. But I believe. And I will trust and follow You.

Amen.

When I'm Not Sure I Should Bother God with This

Not a single sparrow can fall to the ground
without your Father knowing it. And the
very hairs on your head are all numbered.
So don't be afraid; you are more valuable
to God than a whole flock of sparrows.

MATTHEW 10:29–31

LORD, THERE'S A PART OF ME that says I shouldn't even bother You with this prayer.

You're so busy. You've got a whole world to keep spinning, an entire universe to manage, and a few billion people to keep track of.

But then I remember that You know everything, which means You already know what is troubling me. And I suppose if You love me so much that You count the hairs on my head and engrave my name on Your palms, then You won't mind me bringing this to You.

It's not huge in the grand scheme of things. It matters to me, though. And so I dare to believe it matters to You.

Please fix this, Lord.

Fix this situation or fix my heart.

Maybe both. Probably both.

My heart most of all.

And, God? Thank You for never making me feel like I'm bothering You.

Amen.

When I Am Overwhelmed

When he saw the wind, he was afraid and,
beginning to sink, cried out, "Lord, save me!"
Immediately Jesus reached out his hand
and caught him.

MATTHEW 14:30–31, NIV

LORD, THERE IS TOO MUCH. Too many emotions. Too many unknowns.

They're too big and too raw and too real.

And I'm just me.

Unprepared. Ill-equipped. Utterly overwhelmed.

Everyone is looking to me for answers, as if I know what to do. The mental weight of it all is pulling me under, and I . . . I am drowning, Lord.

Reach down and rescue me.

Please.

Amen.

When I'm Afraid
Something Bad Will Happen

I am trusting you, O LORD,
saying, "You are my God!"
My future is in your hands.

PSALM 31:14–15

LORD, I'M WORRIED ABOUT WHAT'S GOING TO HAPPEN. I'm afraid it will not be good.

You hold the future in Your hands, and I know I can entrust it to You . . . but can I confess that I'm still afraid?

Everything is going so well right now. Things are good. And I'm trying to enjoy these blessings You've poured into my life, but there's a part of me that's waiting for the other shoe to drop, for the blessings to end and the disaster to begin.

You're right. I'm making up worries. And the only thing this worrying does is steal pieces of my joy from today.

So. Okay. (Deep breath.) Let me say it again, this time without the fear:

You hold the future in Your hands, and I know I can entrust it to You.

Thank You, God, for listening, for being patient with my worries and fears, and for bringing me back to trusting You.

Amen.

When I Don't Have the Words

If any of you lacks wisdom, you should
ask God, who gives generously to all without
finding fault, and it will be given to you.

JAMES 1:5, NIV

LORD, I FEEL THAT I SHOULD SAY SOMETHING, but I have no idea what that *something* should be.

On my own, with only my words and wisdom, You and I both know that I can easily make a huge mess of things.

Instead of helping, I'm afraid I will hurt.

Lord, fill my mind with just the right words.

Your words.

Words of comfort and compassion.

Words that mend and fix, encourage and uplift.

Words that offer hope, pointing all who hear them to You.

And if words are not what is needed in this moment—if it is some action or simply my presence stepping into and standing alongside—help me know that too.

Amen.

When I Followed God, But . . .

The person who trusts in the LORD will be blessed.
The LORD will show him that he can be trusted.

JEREMIAH 17:7, NCV

GOD, I FOLLOWED YOU. I did exactly what You said to do in Your Word. Or I tried to, at least.

I know You warned me that there would be trouble in this world. That following You would not be the easiest path. But I guess I didn't expect it to be this hard.

If there's something I've done or am doing wrong, show me. I don't think there is, but maybe I'm not seeing things clearly.

Is this a Job sort of moment, God? If it is, I confess that I'm not loving it. But I do love You, and I believe with all my heart that You not only love me but You are also working in my life for my good.

So if this is a test of my faith, then here goes . . .

I trust You, Lord. I believe that Your love and goodness are with me even now in the middle of this. And I believe that Your blessings are waiting for me on the other side of this hardship and hurt.

I'm holding tight to You. I'm going to keep right on holding tight to You as You lead me through this. And I trust that You're holding tight to me too.

I don't understand. But I believe, and I will keep on following You. Because You are the One who overcomes the world.

Amen.

PRAYERS FOR LIFE'S MESSY MOMENTS

When I've Made a Mistake

There is now no condemnation
for those who are in Christ Jesus.

ROMANS 8:1, NIV

LORD, I MADE A MISTAKE.

It wasn't on purpose. I'm not sure it was really a sin (*but please forgive me if it was!*). It was more like a blunder, an oops, an error. Awkward and embarrassing. My cheeks still burn at the memory.

And that's my trouble. I'm not sure anyone else even remembers it. If they do, they probably don't think much of it. But I can't stop thinking about it. It plays over and over again in my mind, like a song stuck on repeat.

I'm tired of reliving it, and I'm tired of shame and regret and if-only-I-hads. Teach me to give myself grace, to release myself from the endless replays, and just move on.

And, God? Thank You for being the One I can bring my mistakes to.

Amen.

When I'm a Mess

If anyone is in Christ, he is a new creation.
The old has passed away; behold, the new has come.

2 CORINTHIANS 5:17, ESV

OH, ABBA . . . I'M LOOKING in the mirror, and I'm seeing a mess. Inside and out.

I've no business coming to You like this except that You invite me to.

So I'm coming, Lord, just as I am. Humbly and even a little fearfully. One big mess, with lots of little messes trailing all around. Clutching Your invitation and daring to believe that You want me here.

With You.

I trust the promise that You are always working in my life and that not one mess of a moment is wasted when I offer it up to You.

Forgive me for all the work I've created for You to do. I'm afraid I'm in need of a full-scale renovation and restoration. Like the Master Carpenter that You are, strip me down to the bare bones of who You originally created me to be.

Bless me with a new beginning. Refreshed, re-created, and renewed in You.

And thank You, Abba, for welcoming a mess like me.

Amen.

When My Heart Needs to Change

Search me, God, and know my heart;
test me and know my anxious thoughts.
See if there is any offensive way in me,
and lead me in the way everlasting.

PSALM 139:23–24, NIV

I THINK I HAVE A HEART PROBLEM, LORD.

Not with its physical rhythm or beat. Rather, I'm feeling out of sync with You.

My heart seems to be filling up with thorns and weeds. And their sharp, cynical bitterness is choking out Your love and my ability to show Your love to others.

Search and sift through my heart, Lord.

Show me my sins and shortcomings—those I've denied and justified and especially those I've hidden even from myself.

Clear away the thorns and weeds. Till the soil of my heart. Nourish it with Your love, and plant Your seeds of truth in it. Grow in me a rich harvest, and help me be ready to share it with everyone I meet.

Amen.

When I've Made a Mess of Things

Purify me from my sins, and I will be clean;
wash me, and I will be whiter than snow.

PSALM 51:7

I MESSED UP, LORD.

I did what You asked me not to do. The very thing I told myself I wouldn't do.

So here we are, and here I am. Needing Your forgiveness once again.

You promise in Your Word that if I confess, You will forgive. So, Lord, I'm here bowing and confessing and humbly daring to claim that promise . . . yet again.

Not because of anything I am owed or have earned but because Your love and grace are so great that You tell me I am welcome here in Your presence. Even when my heart is filthy with sin.

Forgive me.

Wash me clean and make me new.

Make me more and more like You.

Help me not mess up this way again.

And thank You, my Abba, for never giving up on me.

Amen.

When I Need to Remember God's Grace

He brought me out into a spacious place;
he rescued me because he delighted in me.

PSALM 18:19, NIV

LORD, I KNOW WHERE I SHOULD BE.

I remember all too well the things I've done and said—the things that still make me wince and cringe with regret. I know the massive mistakes I've made. And I remember the times I dared to declare I knew better than You . . . and then discovered too late how little I knew.

Yes, You and I both know where I should be. Right smack in the middle of the mess I made for myself.

But I'm not.

Because You reached down and rescued me.

With infinite mercy, incomprehensible grace, and unending love, You've blessed me with this life and these people that I do not deserve.

You've set me down in this broad and spacious place, this lovely life.

Where I can breathe.

Where I can make amends and begin anew.

Where my every breath can be a living praise to You—my Rescuer, my Abba, my Lord.

Help me leave the past where it belongs—with You. And help me remember Your grace.

Amen.

When I've Said Too Much and Can't Reel the Words Back In

Call on me and come and pray to me, and
I will listen to you. You will seek me and find
me when you seek me with all your heart.

JEREMIAH 29:12–13, NIV

LORD, I'VE REALLY PUT MY FOOT IN IT THIS TIME!

My mouth ran so far and so fast ahead of my brain and my prayers that I can't even see the way back to where it began.

Forgive me for allowing the filter of Your love to slip and for saying things I didn't mean. And maybe especially forgive me for saying things I meant but should never have said.

Drench me in Your wisdom, Lord. Soak me through and through. Guide me through figuring out how to fix this mess I've made and repair the damage I've caused with these reckless, thoughtless words.

Please don't let me take one step—or utter one word—without You.

Amen.

When I Act as If It All Depends on Me

I alone am God!
I am God, and there is none like me.
Only I can tell you the future
before it even happens.
Everything I plan will come to pass,
for I do whatever I wish.

ISAIAH 46:9-10

LORD, I REALIZE THAT SOMETIMES I think way too much of myself. I can be guilty of believing that my impact and influence are far greater than they are.

I'm not trying to minimize or put myself down with that statement. Rather, I'm offering myself grace, and I'm reminding myself of my place in this relationship between You and me.

Because sometimes I act as if everything depends on me instead of You. As if my mistakes and shortcomings and shortsightedness will derail Your plans.

How ridiculously arrogant of me.

I'm not big enough or powerful enough to wreck Your plans. In fact, You saw all my "stupids" coming a mile and a millennium away, and You factored them into Your plans.

And, God? I'm so very grateful that it doesn't all depend on me.

Amen.

When I Just Need a Thank-You

Truly I tell you, whatever you did
for one of the least of these brothers
and sisters of mine, you did for me.

MATTHEW 25:40, NIV

LORD, THIS SERVING THING . . . I know it's not supposed to be about me. But right now, I guess I want it to be. At least a little bit.

I've poured so much of my time, my energy, my*self* into others with little to no thanks at all. It's not that I'm serving for the applause. But a simple thank-you would go so far. It would help me know that what I'm doing matters. That it makes some sort of difference in this world.

I'm weary of doing good for those who aren't the least bit grateful!

Oh, wait.

You know all about serving people who aren't the least bit grateful, don't You? People like *me*.

I'm sorry, God. You're right. It's not about me or them. And it's not about any thanks they do or don't give. It's about giving back just a tiny bit of the love You pour out on me.

So, God, how can I thank You by serving those You love—today?

Amen.

When I'm Grateful God Chases After Me

No power in the sky above or in the earth
below—indeed, nothing in all creation will ever
be able to separate us from the love of
God that is revealed in Christ Jesus our Lord.

ROMANS 8:39

LORD, YOU COULD HAVE LEFT ME. You could have thrown up Your hands in frustration and declared that You were done with this wandering one.

But that's not who You are.

That's not who You've ever been.

And it's not who You will ever be.

Always and forever, You are the God who sticks with, chases after, lifts up, and carries home.

You keep coming after Your children. Nothing stops You. Nothing keeps You away.

No matter how far I wander—by neglect or by my own stubborn intention—I never escape Your care.

So I praise You, Abba, with hands and heart lifted high. I praise You for being the God who chases after me.

Amen.

When I Need a Listening Ear

Trust in him at all times, you people;
pour out your hearts to him,
for God is our refuge.

PSALM 62:8, NIV

HI, GOD. IT'S ME AGAIN.

I don't suppose there's anything in particular I wanted to talk about today. I just wanted to . . . well, *talk*. To have someone listen and really hear. Without judgment or interruption. And without me having to worry that my listener will roll their eyes and finally decide I'm far too much trouble after all.

I know I can talk to You. I can spill out all my thoughts and troubles and plans. You'll tell me if I'm off track and nudge me gently back. (Or give me a shove if I don't take Your gentle hint.) You won't leave. Your love won't change. And You won't stop wanting to listen more.

There's no worry about being "too much" or "not enough." I don't have to pretend I am who I am not. I can be me. Because You are always You.

Never changing.

Always loving.

Always listening.

Thank You, Lord, for hearing me.

Amen.

PRAYERS
FOR ALL I'M
FEELING

When Someone Makes Me Laugh

A joyful heart is good medicine.

PROVERBS 17:22, ESV

THANK YOU, GOD.

Thank You for that moment of laughter. It was just what I needed.

And I think You knew that.

I think You sent that person my way, at that very moment, to give me a reason to put down all the burdens, all the worries and cares, and laugh. And not a little giggle or grin but a full laugh-out-loud until my sides ached and I remembered what I had forgotten . . . the renewing power of the simple and uncomplicated joy that comes from You.

Now I feel like I can breathe again.

Like I can face the world again.

This time with a smile and even a little laughter to share.

So thank You, God, for this moment of simple joy and for all the ways You slip into my life and provide exactly what I need, exactly when I need it.

Amen.

When I Hide My Tears

You keep track of all my sorrows.
You have collected all my tears in your bottle.
You have recorded each one in your book.

PSALM 56:8

OH, ABBA, HERE I AM AGAIN.

Slipping away, hiding, and closing the door so that no one will see these tears falling from my eyes and down my face.

Why do I hide my tears, God? Is it because the hurt is too hard to put into words? Or is it because I'm afraid others won't understand? Perhaps it's all those echoes of "Why are you crying?" and "What do you have to cry about?" that bubble up from the past and silence me.

It's not always safe to share my tears, so I've learned to hide them away.

But *You* see, Abba.

You know.

You understand.

Please step in to comfort as only You can, and reach down to dry my tears. Whisper words of courage over me, giving me the strength I need to step out into the world again.

And thank You, Abba, for seeing and counting my tears.

Amen.

When I Just Hate Everything

Let the peace that Christ gives control your
thinking, because you were all called together
in one body to have peace. Always be thankful.

COLOSSIANS 3:15, NCV

CAN I BE HONEST, LORD? I mean, it's not as if I can really lie to You.

It's just that it seems somehow . . . *disrespectful,* I guess, to bring this to You. But You invite me to pray about everything and bring all my cares to You. So here goes . . .

I'm just feeling like I hate everything.

I don't really. I know that, and You know that. But nothing is feeling good or right in this moment. And I hate feeling this way. My mind tells me there is so much in my life to be thankful for. So many good things are happening right this very moment. Yet it's as if all I can see is everything that's going wrong . . . or at least not the way I want it to go.

The truth is that I'm about two seconds away from a full-out pity party that nobody—including me—wants to attend.

Can You help me shake off this mood, this horrible attitude? Maybe whisk it away with a glimpse of Your goodness? Or an avalanche of it? Actually, I suppose that's what You're doing right now as You—Lord Almighty, *El Shaddai*—take time to listen to me and my bad attitude.

So thanks, God. Thank You for being patient with me, even when my moods are all out of whack.

Amen.

When I'm Lonely

Be strong and courageous! Do not be afraid
and do not panic before them. For the
LORD your God will personally go ahead of you.
He will neither fail you nor abandon you.

DEUTERONOMY 31:6

GOD, I KNOW IN MY HEART there's not a moment of my life that has not been lived in Your presence. For that, I thank You. I truly am so grateful for Your nearness. But here's my struggle: Even though You are here with me, I still feel so very *alone*.

Even now, there are people all around me in my life—some I already call friends—but reaching out seems so impossibly hard.

Being vulnerable?

Walking up and starting a conversation?

Opening myself to rejection?

I'm cringing inside. It seems easier to be alone, but . . . then there would still be this loneliness.

Give me the courage to reach out and the confidence to try to connect with someone. Remind me that a smile and kindness and a listening ear go a long way. And help me remember that I'm someone worth getting to know.

After all, You think so.

Amen.

When I'm Grateful for a Friend

Encourage one another and build each
other up, just as in fact you are doing.

1 THESSALONIANS 5:11, NIV

GOD, SOMETIMES I JUST HAVE TO MARVEL at all You've created. Not only mountains and moons and the huge sorts of things. But the little, not-visible-to-the-eye sorts of things that, honestly, turn out to be even bigger and huger. (Is that even a word?)

Like friendship.

How did You know I'd need such a friend?

Someone to laugh with me and share corny inside jokes.

Someone who takes my side but isn't afraid to tell me when I'm wrong.

Someone who assures me it's going to be okay but stays by me when it's not.

Someone to figure out life with.

Someone who challenges me to stay close to You.

Thank You, God, for the gift of my friend. Please help my friendship be a gift to them.

Amen.

When I'm Struggling to Be Patient

Love is patient, love is kind.

1 CORINTHIANS 13:4, NIV

LORD, THERE WAS A TIME, quite a few years ago, when I prayed for patience.

I quickly learned that patience isn't a gift You give; it's a character trait I earn through the opportunities You provide.

So I stopped praying for patience. It seems, though, that You're still answering my prayer because the opportunities for practicing patience are everywhere and all around me.

My already-limited supply is about to run out.

Could You maybe forget I ever prayed for this whole patience thing? No? I was afraid of that. Well, then, I'm going to need some divine intervention with a side of supernatural strengthening today, Lord.

Help me not say exactly what I think or lash out in exasperation. Filter my words and actions through Your love instead. Remind me to offer others the same empathy and understanding You offer me. Even when they're late. Even when they mess up again. Even when they don't do it the way I would do it.

And maybe help me do all this with a lot fewer eye rolls and arched eyebrows—and with a lot more kindness and grace.

Amen.

When I'm Angry

Give your burdens to the LORD,
and he will take care of you.
He will not permit the godly to slip and fall.

PSALM 55:22

ABBA, I'VE COUNTED TO TEN and counted to ten again . . . and then again. But *that* straw might be the one that breaks this camel's back.

The weight of this anger is like a burden I want to hurl away with hurtful words and cutting glares. (You know I'm all too good at those.)

But that's exactly what I *don't* need to do. Not even close. Even if my anger is justified . . . and I'm pretty sure it is! (*Okay. Yes. I might need to work on that attitude a bit.*) So even *if* my anger is justified, I realize that unloading this burden by unleashing my frustrations on others will only make the whole situation so much worse.

So I ask You to take the burden—the weight—of this anger from me.

Cool my temper, and tame my tongue. Open my eyes to see this "last straw" for what it really is. And if it is something to be angry about, help me handle it without adding to the burden by losing my temper. Let my response show everyone how much I love You and how much they are loved by You too.

Amen.

When I've Absolutely Crushed It

May he equip you with all you need
for doing his will.
May he produce in you,
through the power of Jesus Christ,
every good thing that is pleasing to him.

HEBREWS 13:21

I CRUSHED IT TODAY, LORD. I mean *really* crushed it.

The pressure was on, and it was up to me to make it happen. And I did! I nailed it! I was awesome, and it was awesome, and . . . it wasn't actually me at all.

It was You. You crushed it, and You were awesome.

I asked for Your help, Your wisdom, and Your strength, and yet again, You came through. You enabled me to crush it, to nail it, to be awesome.

So while everyone around me today was cheering me on and congratulating me—and while I was patting myself on the back a bit too—I haven't forgotten for one second that . . .

anything good that comes from me most surely started with You.

I'm not saying I'm worthless or no good on my own—Your Word tells me that's not true. But I know that I'm only at my best when I'm in step with You.

So . . . *we* crushed it today, God. And it was all thanks to You.

Amen.

When I Am Incandescently Happy

I will praise the LORD all my life;
I will sing praises to my God as long as I live.

PSALM 146:2, NCV

THANK YOU, GOD.

Thank You for the wonder of this moment, for working all of this out. Thank You for the joy bubbling up inside me.

I can't help but smile and even laugh out loud a little. Why? Because I am so happy.

And You're to blame in the best of ways.

You have so much to do—a whole world full of people and creatures to care for. And yet . . . *and yet,* You prepared this day for me. You set all these pieces in place for me.

Some will chalk it all up to coincidence. Others will say it's because of the work of my own hands and the working out of my own plans. Still others will declare I'm due for a little happiness.

But You and I know the truth, don't we? You prepared this day just for me.

And I am ridiculously, incandescently happy . . . because of You.

Amen.

When I Feel Peaceful

Now may the Lord of peace himself give
you peace at all times in every way.

2 THESSALONIANS 3:16, ESV

LORD, AS I SIT HERE WITH YOU, I am wrapped in a peace that defies understanding. A peace that could only come from Your power and presence.

And I know I am safe here with You.

Outside this little circle of me and You, the world is chaos. Loud, demanding, and clanging.

When it all gets to be too much, I run to You—though I don't have far to travel. I only need to turn and remember that You are with me always.

Because sometimes I still forget.

Forgive me.

Here in the shelter of Your presence, the clamoring of the world fades away and the peace of Your faithfulness seeps in.

In this sacred space, You offer me Your peace. And I praise You, Father, because I find I can truly say that, yes, it is well with my soul.

Here with You.

Amen.

PRAYERS
FOR LOVING
OTHERS WELL

When I Need to Step Out in Love

Walk in the way of love, just as Christ
loved us and gave himself up for us as a
fragrant offering and sacrifice to God.

EPHESIANS 5:2, NIV

LORD, I HAVE AN OPPORTUNITY to make a difference, to show someone what it means to love without seeking any personal gain.

But it will cost me.

Time and energy and possibly money too.

And it's a risk. They might take my help and turn away. Or they might reject me outright.

I know You understand all that I'm thinking and feeling because You stepped out of heaven and out in love to walk the streets of this earth. You risked rejection and, having counted all the costs, acted anyway. And the difference You made in lives, in the world, and in eternity is endless and immeasurable.

Help me, Lord, to follow Your example in my own small way. Please give me the courage to love more like You.

Amen.

When I Shouldn't Say
What I Really Want to Say

Take control of what I say, O Lord,
and guard my lips.

PSALM 141:3

LORD, THERE ARE WORDS SITTING RIGHT HERE on the tip of my tongue that are just itching to storm out into the world. I've captured them here for a moment, long enough to whisper this prayer.

Please help me not say them.

Because You and I both know that they don't need to be said. Nothing good will come from letting them escape. But I need Your help to keep them in and transform them.

Sweep away these sharp words, and replace them with soft ones.

Melt away my anger and frustration, and replace it with understanding and compassion.

Wash away this terrible, awful wish to wound, and replace it with a desire to lift up and encourage.

Help me, Lord, in this moment, to see and love others as You do. Especially with my words.

Amen.

PS: And, God . . . please help my face not say anything awkward or angry either.

When I'm Navigating a Difficult Relationship

Make allowance for each other's faults, and
forgive anyone who offends you. Remember,
the Lord forgave you, so you must forgive
others. Above all, clothe yourselves with love,
which binds us all together in perfect harmony.

COLOSSIANS 3:13–14

LORD, DON'T LET ME MESS THIS UP.

This relationship means a lot to me. Right now, though, this situation we're in is a little complicated, and navigating it is going to be tricky.

I thought we were on the same page. But now it is oh-so-clear that we are not. And I'm not quite sure how to bridge the gap between me and them.

Give me the patience to hear them out and the insight to see things from their point of view—and especially from *Your* point of view.

Slow me down, and help me not to rush in with my own ideas of how to make this right. I don't want to push my will ahead of Yours and ahead of what You would have me do and say.

Season my words with Your love and my actions with Your grace. Help me love them as You love them and as You created them to be . . . not how I want them to be.

So please don't let me mess this up. Somehow and someway use this to draw us closer to each other and closer to You.

Amen.

When Someone Lets Me Down

What [God] says he will do, he does.
What he promises, he makes come true.

NUMBERS 23:19, NCV

LORD, I CAN'T DECIDE whether to be hurt or angry. I guess I'm a little of both.

You already know everything that's happened, but can I just tell You about it anyway? Everything always seems so much clearer when I talk things through with You.

God, I was counting on them, You know? They said they would—*promised* they would. But then they didn't.

And now I'm stuck with not only this mess but also these feelings of frustration and hurt and . . . a fear that I can't ever fully trust them again.

Show me what is true in this situation and what is the heat of the moment. Help me respond as You would—with questions, yes, but also with grace.

And thank You for being the One I can always run to.

The One who does exactly what He says.

The One who keeps every promise He makes.

The One who will never let me down.

Amen.

When I Need to Apologize

Then Peter came to him and asked,
"Lord, how often should I forgive someone
who sins against me? Seven times?"

"No, not seven times," Jesus replied,
"but seventy times seven!"

MATTHEW 18:21–22

I NEED TO APOLOGIZE, GOD. I know I do.

I need to confess that I was wrong and say I'm sorry. But I don't want to.

Their words were thoughtless and uncaring. Their actions were selfish. They hurt me. And I hit back with my own harsh and hasty words.

I'll admit that it felt good, at least for a minute or two. Of course, all I really did was take a little mess and turn it into a big one.

So, yes, I need to apologize. But I'm still convinced I'm right and they're wrong.

You're right, Lord. This isn't about my own sense of justice or pride, is it? And it isn't even about them. It's about You. It's about aligning my heart with Yours.

It's about the One who's forgiven my all-too-often selfish, thoughtless, and hurtful ways. The One who's welcomed me with open arms. The One who, despite all my flaws and wicked ways, has declared to me: *You are mine.*

Soften my hardened heart. Teach me to set aside my stubborn pride and lay down my sharp words. As much as it is up to me, help me mend what is broken.

Because that's what You did—and do—for me.

Amen.

When Someone Is Late

Be kind to each other, tenderhearted,
forgiving one another, just as God through
Christ has forgiven you.

EPHESIANS 4:32

GOD, I WILL READILY CONFESS that waiting on others is not my strength. Yet here I am waiting because someone is late.

My fingers are itching to send the text, to make the call. But I don't want my impatience and frustration to show through. So I wait. Fingers tapping and eyes checking the clock. Waiting for someone to come and meet with me.

Oh . . . wait. I'm getting a glimpse of my own hypocrisy in that thought.

Is this how You feel, God, as You wait for Your people to come and meet with You? As You wait for me?

Forgive me, God. Forgive me for all the times I've kept You waiting.

Who am I to be impatient?

Help me let go of my frustration. Please keep this tardy one safe and guide them through whatever is delaying them. And when they do arrive, help me greet them with welcome and grace. The way You always greet me.

Amen.

When I'm Irritated and on Edge

You will keep in perfect peace
all who trust in you,
all whose thoughts are fixed on you!

ISAIAH 26:3

LORD, THE WHOLE WORLD IS getting on my last nerve.

I'm not even really sure why. My thoughts are dripping with sarcasm and cutting remarks—and honestly, Lord, it's about all I can do to keep them in my head and not let them spill out into words.

My fingers are hammering out a Morse code of irritation. I can feel that my face is set with that "Are you kidding me?" look. And my heart is pounding like a ticking time bomb.

Diffuse the bomb.

Still my fidgety fingers.

Replace my thoughts with Your thoughts and my words with Your words.

Slow my heartbeat as I breathe out the irritation and frustration ... *1* ... *2* ... *3* ... *4* ... and breathe in the peace of Your presence ... *1* ... *2* ... *3* ... *4*.

Keep me here with You, Lord, until You still my internal storm.

Amen.

When a Loved One Doesn't Know God

Surely your goodness and unfailing love will pursue me
all the days of my life,
and I will live in the house of the LORD
forever.

PSALM 23:6

MY ABBA, THIS ONE I LOVE SO MUCH—this one *You* love far more than I ever could—doesn't love You. And it's breaking my heart.

They don't know You. Not the real You.

They're wandering on their own path and believing the nonsense and lies the world says about You. Their eyes are shut tight against You, and their ears are closed. Nothing I say seems to make a dent in their hardened heart.

But You can.

I know it. I've read of how You changed Saul's—Paul's—heart. I know how You lit up the sky and his life and transformed him from a persecutor to a preacher on that Damascus road.

So I'm asking, Abba, for You to meet my loved one on their Damascus road. Chase after them, and light up the skies of their life—so bright that they cannot deny You.

As gently as possible, soften and change and transform their heart so that they come to call You *Abba* too.

Amen.

When Someone I Love Is Hurting

The LORD is close to the brokenhearted;
he rescues those whose spirits are crushed.

PSALM 34:18

FATHER, SOMEONE I LOVE IS HURTING.

I'm doing what I can, but it's not enough. They need You and Your power to make this better.

Scoop them up.

Hold them close.

Put all the broken pieces back together.

Heal the hurts I can see and the ones I don't even know are there. Soothe their fears and their worries. Surround them and wrap them up so tight in Your arms that they can physically feel Your presence. Then fill their heart to overflowing with Your comfort, peace, hope, and love.

This person is part of my heart, God. It hurts to see them struggle. I know Your heart is hurting too. I'm trusting You to take care of them—and me—and to use this hurt to bring us both closer to You.

Amen.

When I Want to Be God's Goodness in the World

You, O Lord,
are a God of compassion and mercy,
slow to get angry
and filled with unfailing love and faithfulness.

PSALM 86:15

FATHER, I SEE YOUR GOODNESS all around me, and I see the way You've poured it out into my own life.

I praise You for that goodness.

But I want to do more than that. I want to tell the world about it. Not only with my words but with my whole life. Help me, Lord, to live a life that reflects Your goodness to everyone who crosses my path. (Yes, even *that* person.)

Fill my heart with compassion for those who are hurting and lost.

Remind me to give the mercy that I've been given.

Don't let my emotions—especially my anger—outrun Your wisdom and grace.

Teach me to love without fail.

And most of all, help me be faithful always in my love for You.

Amen.

PRAYERS
OF JOY
AND PRAISE

When I Watch the Sun Rise

From the rising of the sun to its setting,
the name of the LORD is to be praised!

PSALM 113:3, ESV

GOOD MORNING, GOD.

I lift up my eyes to the sunrise of Your smile as the light chases away the darkness. Clouds shift through an ever-changing palette of pinks and purples. With a stroke of Your will, shimmers of liquid gold race across the sky, ebbing and flowing and transforming into patches of the softest white that dance across a morning blue.

Yours, God, is an artistry I could never re-create.

I breathe in the crispness of this morning air, not yet sullied by the day's demands or my own stubborn determination to push through in my time and my way.

Thank You for this fresh new day rich with opportunities to discover still more of Your wonders, to step into Your presence, and to simply live side by side with You.

I praise You, God, for this beautiful, glorious new day.

Amen.

When I'm Out for a Walk

In his hand is the life of every creature
and the breath of all mankind.

JOB 12:10, NIV

GOD, I'M OUT FOR A WALK TODAY.

It's a regular, ordinary day. No different from so many others. Yet it's as if I'm seeing everything for the first time. Everywhere I turn my eyes, I am awed by this world around me. This world You have made.

The sights, the sounds, the wonderful fresh-air smells—it's as if You created this little glimpse of paradise just for me. And I wonder . . .

Did You have fun? Did You delight in the creation of all this?

What made You decide to give the cardinal a funny little hat and two black eyes? How did You imagine all these different colors for the flowers? How did You know which ones to stripe and which ones to pepper with polka dots?

Thank You, God, for this little glimpse of paradise. And someday, when I stroll through Your redeemed and restored garden with You on the other side of forever, I hope You'll tell me the secrets of how You created it all.

Amen.

When I Look at Those I Love

This is how God loved the world: He gave his
one and only Son, so that everyone who believes
in him will not perish but have eternal life.

JOHN 3:16

THANK YOU FOR THESE PEOPLE You've placed in my life, God.

They fill up my heart until it seems there cannot be space for any more. Then along comes another, and somehow my heart makes room.

Sometimes I simply sit and watch and listen, trying to soak in the joy of their presence and store away the sweet memories. The sound of their laughter and the sight of their smiles. Their unexpected visits, texted hellos, and unprompted hugs are the treasures I collect.

Do You do that too? Do You sometimes simply sit and watch and listen, soaking in the presence of Your people?

When I look at these who are so precious to me, I can feel the love radiating from my heart and shining through my eyes. And I believe it's a little bit like the way You look at me. At each of us.

Amen.

When the Blessing Is Big

Now to him who is able to do immeasurably
more than all we ask or imagine, according
to his power that is at work within us, to him
be glory in the church and in Christ Jesus
throughout all generations, for ever and ever!
Amen.

EPHESIANS 3:20–21, NIV

I ASKED FOR THIS, GOD.

I prayed and knew You would hear me.

I trusted You to answer in Your own perfect time and way.

But *this*? I can't believe You blessed me like this. Well, I mean, I can believe it because I'm looking at the blessing right here in front of me.

You took my offering of faith and returned it to me in a "pressed down, shaken together, and running over" blessing. Bigger and better than anything I could have thought to ask for. More wonderful than I could imagine. Almost too big to believe.

Almost.

This is Your goodness and grace on display. I don't deserve it, Lord, but I'm oh-so-grateful for it.

And for Your love.

And most of all, for You.

Amen.

When God Makes Me Smile

Choose today whom you will serve. . . .
As for me and my family, we will serve the LORD.

JOSHUA 24:15

I CAN'T STOP SMILING, GOD. And I have to stop and say thank You.

I mean, do You see this? Do You see what is happening in this moment? Of course, You see it. You orchestrated everything to create this moment. And maybe it would sound a bit silly to some, but I believe You made it happen just for me.

To see me smile.

Because that, I believe, is the kind of God You are.

A God who delights in delighting His children. A God so powerful that You tell the sun when to set and rise, place rings around Saturn, and spin galaxies on Your finger. And a God so personal that You reach down from those heavens, step into my world, and create this moment for me.

Just to make me smile.

Giving me yet another reason to love You and follow You all the days of my life.

Amen.

When I Find a Moment of Rest in the Busyness

Then Jesus said, "Let's go off by ourselves
to a quiet place and rest awhile." He said this
because there were so many people coming
and going that Jesus and his apostles didn't
even have time to eat.

MARK 6:31

THANK YOU, FATHER, for this moment of rest. You knew exactly what I needed.

I don't mind the busyness. I'm grateful for all the opportunities I have to work and serve. Really, I am.

But I'm also so very grateful for this chance to rest.

To breathe in the peace of Your presence.

To release the stress and worry and hurry.

To be refreshed, renewed, and restored.

Before I'm pulled back into the busyness.

So thank You, Father, for this moment of rest.

Amen.

When I Am Perfectly Content

The boundary lines have fallen for me in pleasant places;
surely I have a delightful inheritance.

PSALM 16:6, NIV

ABBA, I JUST WANTED TO SAY THANK YOU for how lovely my life is. I know You are the One who made it that way and who keeps right on making it that way.

Is everything perfect? No. I don't suppose it will ever be *perfectly* perfect—at least not this side of eternity.

But it is wonderfully good. Because You are endlessly good.

I'm still a little baffled that You take so much time to pour into me. That You are constantly watching over, providing for, sustaining, and loving . . . *me*.

As for those things that aren't quite perfect, I'm trusting You to use them to somehow make me a little bit more like You.

In the meantime, I'm learning—day by day and sometimes moment by moment—that with You by my side, I really do have all that I need.

And I am perfectly content with the way You love me.

Amen.

When I See God at Work

Jesus said to them, "My Father is always at his
work to this very day, and I too am working."

JOHN 5:17, NIV

I SAW THAT, GOD.

That little thing You did—or rather that thing that would be *little* to anyone else. I saw it. And for me, it was huge. Because You reached down from heaven and visibly stepped into my life.

Yes, my mind knows that You are always here and always at work. It's who You are and what You do.

But once in a while, it's as if You send out a little reassurance. A secret message just for me.

Maybe it's a dreaded task made infinitely easier by the touch of Your hand. Or a flash of heavenly insight into the challenge churning in my mind. Or it might be as simple as a sparrow fluttering down to perch nearby, reminding me that just as You care for the least of these, You are surely taking care of me.

And in the heartbeat of an instant, I *know* You are here, and I breathe the holy fragrance of Your presence into my soul.

I don't understand the hows of this moment or why—when You're busy with so many things—You choose to think of me. But I thank You, Lord, for this moment You've created.

This moment of You reaching down to be with me.

Amen.

When I'm Listening to Creation's Song

Let the sea and everything in it shout his praise!
Let the earth and all living things join in.
Let the rivers clap their hands in glee!
Let the hills sing out their songs of joy
before the Lord.

PSALM 98:7-9

IT'S A RETREAT, A REST, and a step away from the ordinary as I sit outside here with You, Lord, in this quiet yet not-so-quiet place.

Here Your creation sings out its own song of praise. The song You taught it to sing.

The wind whistles a deep, low melody; the trees stretch up their branches to clap out a beat; and the birds chime in with their warbling notes.

All I can do is listen.

I am hesitant to interrupt the natural holiness of this moment—this song—with my voice. Yet You remind me it's my voice You long to hear. So I whisper praises to You in my mind, humming in my heart the words of "How Great Thou Art" and knowing You hear. You always hear my praises.

My God, how great Thou art.

Amen.

When I Gaze Up at the Night Sky

When I consider your heavens,
the work of your fingers,
the moon and the stars,
which you have set in place,
what is mankind that you are mindful of them,
human beings that you care for them?

PSALM 8:3–4, NIV

LORD, WHEN I GAZE UP AT THE STARS, I can't begin to count them all. They stretch out—constellation after constellation, galaxy after galaxy, from infinity to eternity—into a vastness that is beyond anything I could ever imagine. You've placed each one precisely where You wanted it to be and called each one by its name.

In the darkness, the stars wink and blink out their never-ending message—a twinkling Morse code reaching to every corner of the globe that declares, "Our God is real and alive! He rules and He reigns!"

It would be so easy for me to feel small, even insignificant, amid all this vastness. A tiny speck on a tiny planet swirling around in one of Your many million galaxies.

But I don't. I don't feel small at all. I lift up my hands and this prayer and all my praise to You.

Because You call me by my name too.

Amen.

PRAYERS
TO PRAY
TOGETHER

A Prayer for Those Without Shelter

He will cover you with his feathers,
and under his wings you will find refuge;
his faithfulness will be your shield and rampart.

PSALM 91:4, NIV

LORD, THE RAIN IS FALLING OUTSIDE. Gentle patters dance their turns with pounding roars. Now and then, lightning illuminates the sky.

It's a beautiful thing to watch from here, where we're safe and warm inside. Sure, we might fuss over the inconvenience of changing plans. Or we could focus on the way You send the rain to wash and nourish the earth.

But right now, as this rain washes down, we think about those who are without shelter today. Without a home to hide away in.

Be their shelter, Lord.

Tuck them under Your wing.

Warm them next to Your heart.

It's so easy to look at their lack of a home and judge. It's even easier to look away. We confess that we've done both of those things.

Forgive us, Lord.

Guide us to be part of the solution. Show us how we can give them Your hope by becoming Your hands and feet.

Amen.

A Prayer for the Sick and Hurting

O LORD, if you heal me, I will be truly healed;
if you save me, I will be truly saved.
My praises are for you alone!

JEREMIAH 17:14

FATHER, IT'S EASY TO TAKE OUR HEALTH FOR GRANTED. To not think twice about going where we want to go and doing what we want to do. To make plans for the future without thought of our bodies holding us back.

But for some, that kind of freedom is a dreamed-of luxury. And it's those—the ones who are sick and hurting—that we lift up to You today.

Because You are *Jehovah-Rapha,* the God who heals.

Whether the sickness lies in their bodies, minds, or spirits, we pray that You would reach down and lay Your healing hand on them. Pour Your strength into them. Light up the shadows of their struggles with the light of Your love. And, above all, make Your presence known so that they know they are not in this battle alone.

We especially lift up to You those closest to us. We lay them in Your healing hands and entrust them to Your care.

Amen.

A Prayer for Our Sabbath

Come with me by yourselves to
a quiet place and get some rest.

MARK 6:31, NIV

FATHER, WITH THE WHOLE WORLD telling us to go, go, go and demanding more, more, and still more, it's kind of amazing that You—the One who never sleeps—tell us to rest.

Because You know us and all our human frailties so well.

You know that when we're tired and overwhelmed and stretched just a little too thin, we are most vulnerable to attack, to slipping into "it's about me" mode and forgetting how very much we need You.

So we thank You for the protection of this command to rest. And we gratefully accept Your invitation to come away with You. Help us leave behind the worries and cares of this world and find peace with You.

Whether that's in quiet stillness alone or in the middle of loving the ones You've placed in our care, use this Sabbath day of rest to restore our souls and draw us closer to You.

Amen.

A Prayer for Those We Love

May the LORD bless you
and protect you.
May the LORD smile on you
and be gracious to you.
May the LORD show you his favor
and give you his peace.

NUMBERS 6:24–26

GOD, THANK YOU FOR THIS LIFE You've given us and for this circle of family and friends You've gathered into our lives to love.

We pray that You would bless each of us—and we thank You for the million and one ways You do exactly that every day. Show us how to be encouragers to everyone in our circle, lifters up and not tearers down. And help us widen our circle and love even more.

Make our hearts a little bit more like Yours today. Hold tight to us, and help us hold tight to You. Keep us safe in the embrace of Your grace always.

Be a hedge of protection around us. Cast away any darkness, and flood our lives with the light of Your love. Let it shine so brightly in and through us that the whole world knows . . .

we belong to You.

Amen.

A Prayer for Those We Struggle to Love

Pray for one another.

JAMES 5:16, ESV

COULD WE ADMIT THAT WE are lifting up this prayer rather reluctantly, Lord? And could we confess that there are times we don't really want to ask for this at all?

You know what they've done to us and said about us.

But You tell us to love our enemies. To pray for them and bless them. So we're asking.

Enemy might be too strong a word. There's no actual battlefield. (*Though it sure feels like one!*) Instead of dodging bullets, we're dodging cutting words and behind-the-back verbal attacks. Even so, we don't hate them like an enemy. We'd just rather not be around them.

Something must be going on in their life, Lord. Some reason they're behaving this way. If it's something we're doing, show us and help us fix it, if it needs fixing.

In the meantime, heal whatever hurt or fear or insecurity is making them act this way. Change their heart. And ours could probably use some work too.

Friendship seems an impossibility—though we know better than to use that "impossible" word with You. But we'd love to have peace in this relationship, and that can only come through You.

Amen.

A Prayer for the Brokenhearted

He tends his flock like a shepherd:
He gathers the lambs in his arms
and carries them close to his heart.

ISAIAH 40:11, NIV

LORD, YOU ARE THE GREAT SHEPHERD. You know Your sheep. And though our numbers are like the stars in the sky, You call each of us by name.

You know our comings and our goings and all the details of our lives. And so You know when one of Your sheep is hurting. You know when a heart has been broken.

Go to that one, Abba, and gather them up in Your arms, just as You promise in Your Word. Let Your presence be so tangible and so real that they *feel* Your arms surrounding them.

Hold them close to Your own heart and love away the hurt.

Mend what was broken.

Whisper reminders of who they really are: Your beloved child.

Hold tight to them until they can stand once again—and then forever after.

Amen.

A Prayer for When It's Time
to Relax and Play

This is the day that the Lᴏʀᴅ has made;
let us rejoice and be glad in it.

PSALM 118:24, ESV

FATHER, THANK YOU FOR THIS DAY You've given us away from the rush and crush of the ordinary. For this chance to laugh and play and simply have fun together.

Help us not to waste time or thoughts on worries of what we could be doing or guilt over what we "should" be doing.

Teach us to embrace this time away.

To entrust all the coulds and shoulds to Your perfect care.

To relax in this different kind of rest—not still and quiet but busy doing the things that make our hearts smile.

Help us be patient with one another amid our differences and give grace. Bless our time together so that it strengthens our relationships with one another and with You.

Thank You, Abba, for this time to play.

Amen.

A Prayer for Boldness

Don't worry about how to respond
or what to say. God will give you the
right words at the right time.
For it is not you who will be speaking—
it will be the Spirit of your Father
speaking through you.

MATTHEW 10:19–20

NOW IS NOT THE TIME to be silent or shy. We know that, God. Now is the time to be bold.

To take risks.

To stand up for those who cannot.

To speak out for those who have no voice.

But, God, we're going to need Your help to do that. Because it's risky and because we're more than a little afraid of what we might lose. Please be with us in this.

Fill our hearts with Your courage and our resolve with Your strength.

Drench us in Your wisdom.

Flood our minds with Your thoughts and the words You would have us speak.

And cover us with Your hand of protection.

Let us be far less worried about what others might think and far more concerned about what matters to You. Please help us be bold for You.

Amen.

For Daddy—thank you for buying me that first
computer and for cheering me on ever since.

And for Abba, always.

Ink & Willow

An imprint of the Penguin Random House
Christian Publishing Group, a division of
Penguin Random House LLC

1745 Broadway, New York, NY 10019

inkandwillow.com

penguinrandomhouse.com

All Scripture quotations, unless otherwise
indicated, are taken from the Holy Bible, New
Living Translation, copyright © 1996, 2004, 2015
by Tyndale House Foundation. Used by permission
of Tyndale House Publishers, Carol Stream, Illinois
60188. All rights reserved. Scripture quotations
marked (ESV) are taken from the ESV® Bible (The
Holy Bible, English Standard Version®), copyright
© 2001 by Crossway, a publishing ministry of Good
News Publishers. Used by permission. All rights
reserved. Scripture quotations marked (NCV) are
taken from the New Century Version®. Copyright
© 2005 by Thomas Nelson. Used by permission.
All rights reserved. Scripture quotations
marked (NIV) are taken from the Holy Bible,
New International Version®, NIV®. Copyright
© 1973, 1978, 1984, 2011 by Biblica Inc.™ Used
by permission of Zondervan. All rights reserved
worldwide. (www.zondervan.com). The "NIV"
and "New International Version" are trademarks
registered in the United States Patent and
Trademark Office by Biblica Inc.™ Scripture
quotations marked (NKJV) are taken from the New
King James Version®. Copyright © 1982 by Thomas
Nelson. Used by permission. All rights reserved.

Copyright © 2025 by Tama Fortner

Penguin Random House values and supports
copyright. Copyright fuels creativity, encourages
diverse voices, promotes free speech, and creates
a vibrant culture. Thank you for buying an
authorized edition of this book and for complying
with copyright laws by not reproducing, scanning,
or distributing any part of it in any form without
permission. You are supporting writers and
allowing Penguin Random House to continue to
publish books for every reader. Please note that
no part of this book may be used or reproduced in
any manner for the purpose of training artificial
intelligence technologies or systems.

INK & WILLOW and colophon are registered
trademarks of Penguin Random House LLC.

INTERIOR ILLUSTRATIONS: shutterstock.com:
Merfin, botanical florals (page 20); **Roisa,** abstract
florals and shapes (pages 6, 20, 31, 64, 86, 119);
Don_ya, abstract florals and shapes (pages 9, 42,
64, 97, 108); **Tanya Syrytsyna,** abstract florals and
shapes (pages 9, 53, 64, 75, 108, 119)

The Library of Congress catalog record is available
at http://lccn.loc.gov/2024034759.

Printed in China

9 8 7 6 5 4 3 2 1

First Edition

The authorized representative in the EU
for product safety and compliance is Penguin
Random House Ireland, Morrison Chambers,
32 Nassau Street, Dublin D02 YH68, Ireland.
https://eu-contact.penguin.ie

BOOK TEAM: Editor: Leslie Calhoun • Production
editor: Jessica Choi • Managing editor: Julia
Wallace • Production manager: Maggie Hart •
Copy editor: Kristen Defevers • Proofreaders:
Tracey Moore, Karissa Silvers

BOOK DESIGN BY Jessie Kaye and Zaiah Antwi

COVER ART: shutterstock.com: **Merfin,** botanical
florals; **Roisa,** abstract florals; **Dmitr1ch,** woven
texture

For details on special quantity discounts for bulk
purchases, contact
specialmarketscms@penguinrandomhouse.com.